LEADING EDGE
CONTROL
TECHNOLOGY
by
RUPERT M LOYDELL

NEWTON-LE-WILLOWS

Published in the United Kingdom in 2013
by The Knives Forks And Spoons Press,
122 Birley Street,
Newton-le-Willows,
Merseyside,
WA12 9UN.

ISBN 978-1-909443-12-9

Copyright © Rupert M Loydell, 2013.

The right of Rupert M Loydell to be identified as the author of this work has been asserted by him in accordance with the Copyrights, Designs and Patents Act of 1988. All rights reserved. No part of this publication may be reproduced, stored in a retrieval system, transmitted in any form or by any means, electronic, photocopying, recording or otherwise, without prior permission of the publisher.

Acknowledgements:

Some of these poems first appeared in *The Construction of Memory (Download Poems), The Delinquent, Gists & Piths, Mimesis*.

Table of Contents

1. LEADING EDGE CONTROL TECHNOLOGY

Hairy, Spiny, Naked	7
Indices, Scores, Grids	8
Isolate, Mark, Omit	9
Frame, Scale, Select	10
Tracing, Projection, Survey	11
Project, Index, Distance	12
Transfer, Codify, Analyse	13
Route, Network, Flow	14
Organise, Mask, Orientate	15
Collect, Combine, Connect	16

2. RADIAL SONGBOOK

Tribal Enticement	19
Memory Moon	20
Prayer Rug Exorcism	21
Three Perspectives & a Short Scenario	23
The Greenhouse in Winter	24

LEADING EDGE
CONTROL TECHNOLOGY

> Look, who can say what these things mean?
> They make patterns in our lives and all I know
> Is not knowing helps, but I couldn't tell you why.
>
> – 'Don't Ask', Yannis Ritsos
> (tr. David Harsent)

HAIRY, SPINY, NAKED

This is not a breathless account of brave new discoveries;
a covering of fine hairs can control the temperature too.

Here is a vehicle for explaining light and illumination,
a glass of beer to help us understand the problem of liquids.

One is tempted to wonder why dry land was colonised at all;
how little we know about the process that made it possible.

Let it be awful and awkward and wrong,
almost useless for relating structure to function;

adaptation exploits possibilities as best it can,
mitigating rather than harvesting the effect.

The whole structure is supported by a network
of finest crystal and maximum effervescence,

whose sources are trans-historical and multicultural,
a radical development in science at the time.

INDICES, SCORES, GRIDS

The instructions are a bit confusing and tucked away
but additional verification can be obtained
by requesting a copy of the bonus report.

The scoring mechanism presents a novel view of risk,
a nine-square grid that provides a graphical parameter estimation
using search within a target to implement functionality.

Kills made within each band will generate the same extra score;
the emergent poles must always have either a high or a low.
Press to disable hints, click here for an explanation why.

ISOLATE, MARK, OMIT

It takes precisely twenty days to fell the tree
and fourteen to remove the branches.
Mark a scene as omitted and it disappears from your script.

To remove stored fat, do the least necessary;
for read-only and ambiguous cursors,
slide the adaptor slowly down the column.

Avoid electric shock or energy hazards,
too much ambiguity or omission.
(A term fittingly applied to sins.)

Come with me privately to a place
where you will see an isolated bridge device:
dramatic, well-constructed and lots of fun.

I've used that more or less
as an ingenious solution to the troubles
and in order to confound any sense of orientation.

FRAME, SCALE, SELECT

Is there a way I can refresh the clips
so that they scale when dropped?
I must have changed a setting unknowingly,
there are no handles to pull.
Can auto-self be permanently disabled?

Take a video of an object in motion,
move the current-time indicator to a location;
keep in mind that you're not limited
to specifying percentages,
make sure the picture content is selected.

Now you can move, size, and rotate;
shift-drag layer handle, package preflight
map surrounds, frames and graticules,
and transform aspects of perceived reality.
Try to select static as a continuous buffer.

TRACING, PROJECTION, SURVEY

Every plane through the origin intersects the unit sphere
and reproduces the shape and substance of an object,

but as the transducers do not transmit in all directions,
the acoustic energy is projected into the water.

It is necessary to carry out a triangulation of the territory:
trace, trace out, trace over, map, trigger and tune in.

Radiance of any light in space can always be obtained
by tracing the axial plane and plunge.

It has to be done in solid Earth at the stratigraphic level,
with unaliased spatial trace interpolation in the f-k domain.

Once the conjunction is completed we lose
any trace of inferred presupposition.

Imagine wrapping a piece of paper around a globe
and tracing where the paper touches the surface.

Well, I imagine tracing paper would be too expensive,
always use a calculator to complete multiple choice.

PROJECT, INDEX, DISTANCE

Test your ability to judge short and long distance.
The mode of delivery is now in transition, moving towards
a star at a distance d which has a total power output of p.
Consider what you see when you limit your information:

The stopping distance of a vehicle is the sum of
blast area and quantity distance considerations,
because the spatial index of traditional geometry fields
cannot be used. Shooting distance affects damage

and is instrumental in stopping the fire from jumping
from the micro to the macro and then to the mega.
The perpendicular distance between adjacent planes
is related to the quest for cheaper housing.

There are too many pictures here, but if you want more,
the contact and fly ball rates are pretty easy to project.
The only thing I'm missing is the front distance sensors
to measure the spread of your influence and reputation.

TRANSFER, CODIFY, ANALYSE

If a choice of law rule for fraud is codified,
what should it say and how should it say it?
Codification is not mere transport of what exists
in human brains to another agent;
effective sharing of tacit knowledge
generally requires extensive personal contact.

Time series analysis is a branch in the field,
econometrics is maintaining the cemetery.
Network structure and knowledge transfer
in cluster evolution analyse the paradoxes
for organizational learning in schools:
intelligence essentials for everyone.

ROUTE, NETWORK, FLOW

In theory, a flow network is a directed
optimal lane-based evacuation route.

Traffic flows proactively onto multiple paths,
colours display the severity of firewalls in place.

The paradox is on a different machine
where blind windows overlook the sea.

ORGANISE, MASK, ORIENTATE

I've been able to fill my time and fit right in. I organise
small activities and big games, can animate camp fires
and lead meditations. Come and help me tell the stories
hidden behind the masks or invent totally new ones,
help me assign team names and finalise assessment.

Activity in general is a property of the animate form,
a matter of routine to orientate behavior towards telling the truth,
a direct strategy to help the community and the people that live
in that community create some basic materials and use them in
explorative song cycles and to help organise themselves.

Emotions like love and grief glissade across the mask of childhood,
leaving traces of unmediated vital praxis within the capitalist mode.
To see or wear an oxygen mask in your dreams suggests that
you are feeling sensitive in regard to the whole question
of secret, atheistic organisations, their origin and nature.

COLLECT, COMBINE, CONNECT

The inhabitants of a town, being collected into one place, can easily combine together. Distance-based clustering is done by removing clues. Smaller submodels can be added to a main model, combining information from other sources with the original information. Read through all the features in a workspace, think for a moment about all the factors: otherwise it's just a collection of meaningless words.

Various collecting ducts within the medullary pyramids merge to form papillary channels, which drain to a portal, and also release substances that are secreted into the tubule to combine with sight distance and spot improvements. The existing road is ideal for bicyclists who are riding to somewhere else but we don't like people who mention f-zero or are devoted to animals obtained by black market trade.

Collect the red rag, as well as the blue jumper on the floor in between the two largest boxes. Bring these ingredients to their delivery point and use the exposed bare metal of the electrical wires to connect theM You must not include functionality that proxies or the memory accounting features of this leading-edge control technology. Those two steps help save money on labour. Thank you for being a customer.

TRIBAL ENTICEMENT

TRIBAL ENTICEMENT

He was eardropping on
the spiral paths of flicker

Half light summer invocation
Perfunctory dream envelopes

A lne of shadow between
floating plastic conventions

Deliberate language
Grey entry shriek

MEMORY MOON

shadows on the water
                    widower

circular breathing
                    monkey talk

perception of distance
                    short summary

threadbare futures
                    golden years

perfect circle
                    wave goodbye

the longest day
                    sudden monsoon

PRAYER RUG EXORCISM

architectural conjugate alphabet autobus
carbonium agony barrington coddle
celebrant blowfish constrictor assess

craftsmen dichloride alias avowal
citizen breastwork delirious champagne
apartheid designate daredevil chuckwalla

autumn compromise calamity din
desolate avalanche clamorous backscatter
diminutive curfew bimetal cassette

cyanate confederacy bluebonnet access
alloy detention carbonium backlog
crescent bestowal detergent complaint

anheuser cryptographer corpulent agent
bloodline coalition cutover bounce
bookplate contestant communicant chord

coercible ballad census aversion
coolheaded convulsive artillery concuss
destinate chorus airmail bookend

discriminate crossbar brickbat amphora
bleary demurring charcoal abutt
chairperson coverage abnormal convene

bedstraw commensurate crankcase consortium
deliberate ascension congestive crossover
arduous bedtime commando child

creekside dispersal blueprint affect
bucolic appliance automate dog
dizzy antennae cherry critique

bricklaying discovery   dahlia convention
   amputee congress   demented dog
  audience continuum   chauffeur crosscut

   auto decouple   commodious acute
 congruent cheekbone   analeptic balm
 additive discussion   cholesterol deface

 barefaced alarm   adventitious congestion
   catheter audit   appropriate criteria
  buoyant condolence   asterisk charm

  artificial certainty   bistable crack
   deluded blather   archaic crush
  cognac choreography   dervish consent

 commensurate addition   ceremonial aunt
  assonant compression   attitude cult
  bowstring combustible   bubble burlap

  asbestos conversion   buckwheat companion
  benzedrine aspirate   conspiracy browse
   aqueduct casebook   deadwood chemise

    cybernet diction   disruptive dirge
  asphalt beneficiary   candlestick bitter
   askance contention   countryside burn

THREE PERSPECTIVES
& A SHORT SCENARIO

Golden age, hook & eye:
beauty knows no pain.

Specific shape of the ape:
epileptic seizure comparison.

Time blades, sheet almanac:
chaos of stars, critical mass.

Ducks & drakes, memorial flag:
footprints into the future.

THE GREENHOUSE IN WINTER

residual subsidy
shaggy arrogate
chicory terminal

kosher cistern
inactive literacy
baldpate dogma

sedition elapse
glaucoma swordtail
adoptive trustee

hillcrest transduction
fallible costume
dihedral arcade

arcane reversion
incomprehension
personal fault

atlantic electorate
hidden bucolic
anthracite pain

orthicon stricture
diagram culture
penultimate glass

glossolalia hobby
mimetic envoy
autonomous gold

electoral purgation
crematory hideout
wanting to kiss your neck